4th Laugh -a- Minute Joke Book

by
Gene Perret
Illustrated by
Sanford Hoffman

Sterling Publishing Co., Inc.   **New York**

To
Dick and Tess
for the wonderful
gift they gave me

Library of Congress Cataloging-in-Publication Data

Perret, Gene.
   Laugh-a-minute joke book / Gene Perret: illustrated by Sanford
Hoffman.
       p.   cm.
   Includes index.
   Summary: A collection of jokes about the many aspects of growing
up, grouped under such headings as "It's All Relatives" and "Hard Times
in School."
   ISBN 0-8069-7414-1
   1. Wit and humor, Juvenile.   2. Children—Juvenile humor.
3. Children—Conduct of life—Juvenile humor. [1. Jokes.]
I. Hoffman. Sanford, ill. II. Title.
PN6163.P46   1991
818'.5402—dc20
                                90-27674
                                   CIP
                                   AC

10 9 8 7 6 5 4 3 2

© 1991 by Gene Perret
Published by Sterling Publishing Company, Inc.
387 Park Avenue South, New York, N.Y. 10016
Distributed in Canada by Sterling Publishing
℅ Canadian Manda Group, P.O. Box 920, Station U
Toronto, Ontario, Canada M8Z 5P9
Distributed in Great Britain and Europe by Cassell PLC
Villiers House, 41/47 Strand, London WC2N 5JE, England
Distributed in Australia by Capricorn Ltd.
P.O. Box 665, Lane Cove, NSW 2066
Manufactured in the United States of America
All rights reserved

Sterling ISBN 0-8069-7414-1 Trade
             0-8069-7415-X Paper

CONTENTS

1.
IT'S ALL RELATIVES

COMING, MOTHER:

You know, we have National Peanut Butter week in this country. How's that for being ungrateful? We give a whole week to peanut butter and only one day to Mother.

Of course, mothers don't go that good with jelly.

★　　★　　★

My Mom's tough. Once when she said "no," I said, "Jimmy's mother always lets him do it." I got sent to my room. Jimmy and his mother got sent to their rooms, too.

★　　★　　★

It never pays to get fresh with my Mom. She knows where I live.

★　　★　　★

Mothers make sure we do what's right. They're like the traffic cop on the highway of life.

★　　★　　★

My Mother is very forgetful. I was two and a half years old when I was born.

★　　★　　★

Every time I tell my Mom I lost something, she says, "Where did you put it last?" I say, "Mom, if I knew that, it wouldn't be lost."

★　　★　　★

My Mother is so neat, if I get up to go to the bathroom in the middle of the night, when I come back, my bed is made.

★　　★　　★

My Mom puts starch in everything. Once I sneezed and cut my nose on my handkerchief.

★　　★　　★

My brother once fell out of bed and broke his pajamas.

★　　★　　★

One time I got so mad at my Mom that I wanted to run away from home, but I didn't. There aren't too many places you can go when you're not allowed to cross the street.

★　　★　　★

FATHER
AND FARTHER:

Dads know everything there is to know about sports—until you let them play in the Father-Son game.

★   ★   ★

My Dad's always hollering at me what to do when I play Little League. I don't stand outside his office window and yell at him how to write letters to his clients.

★   ★   ★

Fathers work very hard for their money. At least, that's what they'll tell you any time you ask them for some of it.

★   ★   ★

Not too many kids know what their fathers are doing at work. Some of the fathers don't, either.

★   ★   ★

Fathers can read the paper and carry on a conversation at the same time. The problem is when they're done they know neither what they read nor what they said.

★　★　★

My Dad likes to help me with my homework. Oh sure, it takes me a little longer, but . . .

★　★　★

Dads are pretty good at history. That's because they were there when most of it happened.

★　★　★

My Dad knows everything there is to know about everything—even if it is different from what they teach us at school.

★　★　★

I never correct my Father when he gives me wrong answers with my homework. I'm sure he'll learn the right answer when he gets a little older, anyway.

★　★　★

MY BROTHER'S BAD DRIVING:

When my brother passes people on the street, they're not called "pedestrians;" they're called "survivors."

★   ★   ★

My brother's a very unpredictable driver. He has a bumper sticker that says, "I brake for absolutely no reason at all."

★   ★   ★

When my brother puts his arm out to make a signal, the only thing you can be sure of is that the window is open.

★   ★   ★

My brother is such a bad driver, when he went to get his license, he got four tickets on the written test alone.

★   ★   ★

My brother does so many terrible things when he drives that we have to convert the trunk of our car to a penalty box.

★   ★   ★

The only thing more scary than going out for a ride with my brother is going out "trick or treating" with Freddy Krueger.

★   ★   ★

When I go for a ride with my brother he says, "Do you want to sit in the front?" I say, "No thanks. I'll kneel and say my prayers in the back."

. . . If I sit up front with him, I might be considered an accomplice.

★   ★   ★

My brother figures he doesn't have to obey the rules of the road, because most of the time he drives on the sidewalk.

★   ★   ★

My brother once got a ticket for parking on two roads at the same time—Mr. and Mrs. Roads.

. . . They were in their dining room at the time.

The policeman said, "How did you get in their dining room?" My brother said, "I turned left at their kitchen."

★   ★   ★

The other night my brother came home and Dad said, "Where did you leave the car?" My brother said, "It's parked in the alley." Dad said, "Our street doesn't have an alley." My brother said, "It does now."

★   ★   ★

I'll give you an idea how badly my brother drives. When he puts the key in the ignition, the hood ornament screams and runs away.

★   ★   ★

I'll give you an idea how bad my brother's driving is. If he drove a getaway car, the bank robbers would rather stay behind and get captured.

. . . and they'd be safer, too.

★   ★   ★

Once my brother drove the wrong way on a one-way street. I said, "Do you know where you're going?" He said, "Yeah, but I must be late. Everybody else seems to be going home."

★   ★   ★

My brother is more dangerous with a car than he would be with a loaded gun. A gun doesn't seat four passengers.

★   ★   ★

When you ride with my brother, you not only fasten your seat belt, you also make out your last will and testament.

★   ★   ★

A safe drive with my brother means you finish in the same car you started in.

★   ★   ★

My brother drives fast. He says he wants to get home before all the accidents happen.

★   ★   ★

MY GRANDPA'S SMELLY CIGARS:

I have a grandpa who smokes smelly cigars. His cigars smell so bad that when he smokes them, even he has to go into another room.

★   ★   ★

When he comes to our house, Mom gives us a choice—"Do you want to visit with your grandpa, or do you want to breathe?"

★   ★   ★

We always know when he's coming to visit us. Our smoke alarms go off three days before he gets here.

★   ★   ★

When he smokes at our house, skunks come to our door to complain.

★   ★   ★

That smell gets into everything. When he comes to our house, our dog takes her fur off.

★   ★   ★

My Mom has thrown out meals that smelled better than that.

★   ★   ★

My grandpa's cigars are powerful. One visit from him is like three visits from the fumigator.

★   ★   ★

My grandpa was there when I spoke my first words—"P.U."

★   ★   ★

His cigars smell so bad that one day our trash compactor caught fire—and it smelled better.

★   ★   ★

His cigars smell so bad that if your hands are busy, your nose will hold itself.

★   ★   ★

His cigars smell so bad, when he comes to visit, our smoke alarms move to a neighboring state.

My grandpa likes to run his fingers through my sister's curly hair. What he doesn't realize is that her hair was straight before he lit his cigar.

★   ★   ★

UNCLE LOUIE'S GOOFY INVENTIONS:

My uncle crossed an ordinary house mouse with an elephant. Know what he got? A letter of resignation from the cat.

★　　★　　★

My Uncle Louie crossed a cat with Limburger cheese. Whatever it is he got smells terrible, but it catches mice like crazy.

★　　★　　★

My Uncle Louie tried to end the smog problem by crossing gasoline with peanut butter. All the exhaust sticks to the roof of your tailpipe.

★　　★　　★

My uncle invented a spray can with eight holes in it. Now he's working on a deodorant for octopuses.

* * *

My uncle crossed a tortoise with a hare. Now nobody'll race it.

* * *

My Uncle Louie invented a combination electric toothbrush-electric razor. You know what he got? Cavities in his beard.

. . . and his gums got a five o'clock shadow.

* * *

My uncle crossed a rubber tree with a coconut tree. He was trying to get a basketball that you could eat.

* * *

My Uncle Louie crossed a time bomb with a Timex watch. Even after it explodes, it keeps on ticking.

* * *

My uncle crossed a pack of cigarettes with a pack of crayons. He says they taste terrible, but the stains on his fingers are beautiful.

* * *

My Uncle Louie invented an airplane that flies on onion juice. It's not only cheaper, but it never has any trouble getting cleared for take-off.

* * *

2.
THEY'RE ANIMALS!

OUR DOG:

We own a big dog. If you want to hit him on the nose with a newspaper, you have to stand on a chair.

★ ★ ★

He's a cross between a Great Dane and a '72 Buick.

★ ★ ★

This dog is so big he not only chases cars; he catches them.

★ ★ ★

It's hard to control a dog this big. He takes *us* to obedience school.

★ ★ ★

This dog is so big and frightening, the mailman won't come near our house. He mails us our mail.

★   ★   ★

We put up a sign that said, "Beware of Dog," but he ate it.

★   ★   ★

This dog loves children. He thinks they're delicious.

★   ★   ★

You wonder what a dog this big eats? Anything that's near him when he's hungry.

★   ★   ★

It's not really a dog. It's a fur covered appetite.

If you leave anything on the floor, he eats it. We didn't realize this until one day we came home and the sofa was missing.

★   ★   ★

We used to have wall-to-wall rugs until one day we came home and found the dog with wall-to-wall indigestion.

Every night the dog brings my Dad his pipe, his slippers, and the newspaper. For the next half-hour we all sit around and try to figure out which is which.

★   ★   ★

We have no control over this animal. We wanted a pet, but he has us under house arrest.

★   ★   ★

If this dog likes you, he doesn't lick your hand; he lets you live.

★   ★   ★

We bought him as a watch dog, but now we don't need him for that. It costs so much to feed him, we have nothing left for burglars to steal.

★   ★   ★

And this dog is mean—really mean. He wears a black leather jacket and motorcycle boots.

★   ★   ★

The dog can be vicious, but friendly, too. He wags his tail while he's biting yours.

★   ★   ★

You've heard of dogs whose bark is worse than their bite? Well, this mutt's breath is worse than his bite.

★   ★   ★

And the dog is not real smart. He sits when we tell him to, but we have to show him which end to use.

★   ★   ★

He's so dumb, it's a good thing he's big. He got through obedience school on a football scholarship.

★   ★   ★

OUR CAT:

We have the laziest cat in the world. She catches mice by appointment only.

★　★　★

If you want her to catch mice, you have to mix them in with her regular food.

★　★　★

Our cat is so fat, it can only chase mice that have recently been hurt in skiing accidents.

★　★　★

You know it's unfair. Our dog's job is to protect us from burglars and dangerous intruders; our cat's job is to protect us from mice.

★　★　★

Our cat just doesn't like to catch mice. She says she prefers seafood.

★　★　★

Our cat is a very fussy eater. She only likes one brand of canned cat food, and even then she wants to know who packed it.

★　★　★

If she doesn't like the meal, she just doesn't eat it. That's probably why she very rarely gets invited out to dinner.

★　★　★

Sometimes we serve her table scraps and she refuses to eat them. That's kind of an insult to those of us who do.

★　★　★

Our cat does nothing but lie around the house all day. She's just something else that has to be dusted.

Our cat is solid black. She was too lazy to carry around *two* colors.

★ ★ ★

Our cat doesn't bother to chase mice. She'd rather just lie around the house and wait for the goldfish bowl to break.

★ ★ ★

All our cat does around the house is eat, sleep, and get petted. If she ever runs away, I'm going to ask my Mom if I can have that job.

She doesn't respond to affection like a dog does. She figures it takes less energy to be aloof than to wag her tail.

She figures if you enjoy petting her so much, you'll wag *your* tail.

Cats are different from dogs. You can play "fetch" with a cat, but you'll have to go get the stick yourself.

★ ★ ★

Ours is a very mean cat. Of course, you'd be mean, too, if you had to wash yourself all over every day with your own tongue.

★ ★ ★

MY SISTER'S DATES:

You should see some of the guys my older sister dates. I think she belongs to the "Geek of the Month" club.

★   ★   ★

We never know whether she's going to say, "I'd like you to meet my date" or "Can I keep this thing as a pet? It followed me home."

★   ★   ★

Some of her dates, I don't know whether to shake their hand, or try to teach them tricks.

★   ★   ★

Some of her dates are so strange, they look like they were made by the Cub Scouts.

★   ★   ★

I don't know why my sister dates these guys—unless she's thinking of forming her own freak show.

★   ★   ★

We have a little aquarium at home with a fake treasure chest on the bottom. When my sister brings a date home, the fish all go into the trunk and slam the lid shut.

★   ★   ★

Our family dog is a good judge of people, too. My sister came home with one date, and the dog took the family car and drove to Pittsburgh.

Then she dated one guy who had long hair, a beard, and wore sandals. When she brought him home, I didn't know whether to shake his hand, or ask him to perform a miracle.

★   ★   ★

This guy had long hair that fell down in front and met his beard. At first glance, his nose looked like a bald spot.

★   ★   ★

I suppose she kissed him goodnight, but I don't know how. It would take a half-hour to find his mouth.

She came home with one guy who wore black leather boots, black leather pants, and a black leather motorcycle jacket. He looked like a human black jack.

She dated another guy who did nothing but eat. He could finish off an entire cake by himself . . . while it was baking.

He came to the house one day and I said, "My sister's not home." He said, "Good. I'll eat her share."

You've heard of people who eat and run? This guy would eat and eat.

She also dated a big, dumb football player. His muscles were so big he could hardly get his helmet on.

He was so dumb—when he earned his varsity letter, someone had to read it to him.

He was injured one time when the coach gave him the ball and told him to run around his own end.

★   ★   ★

3.
THE STORY OF MY LIFE

GETTING UP
IN THE MORNING:

I hate to get up in the morning. I'd like to climb into a water bed and never get out of it until all the liquid evaporates.

★ ★ ★

MOM: What time do you want to get up in the morning?

KID: I don't want to get up in the morning. I'd rather get up in the afternoon.

★ ★ ★

I can't wake up in the morning until I splash some cold water on my face. The only way I can get up in time for school is to sleep in the sink.

★ ★ ★

My Mother says I'm almost impossible to get out of bed in the morning, so she hooked my bed up to the toaster. Now after three minutes I pop out of bed and land on a plate in the kitchen.

★　★　★

My father keeps telling me that the early bird catches the worm. If I get out of bed early in the morning, I want something better for it than a worm.

★　★　★

One kid kept complaining about headaches. His father said, "How many times do I have to tell you? When you get out of bed in the morning, it's feet first."

★　★　★

My uncle always slept as late as he could. As long as he lived he never knew there were two 8 o'clocks in the same day.

★　★　★

Farmers always get up with the cows. If I was a farmer I'd only buy cows that liked to sleep late.

MY MESSY ROOM:

Let me describe my room to you. It has a bed, a chest of drawers, and everything else in the world in it.

★　　★　　★

I haven't straightened my room in so long I forget what color the rug is.

★　　★　　★

I straightened up my room once and found a younger brother I never knew I had.

★　　★　　★

If my room was a neighborhood, they'd condemn it and put up a slum.

★　　★　　★

I was going to straighten my room yesterday, but I couldn't find the rake and shovel.

★   ★   ★

Mom says my room looks like a cyclone hit it, but that's not true. If a cyclone hit it, it would be neater.

★   ★   ★

I'll give you an idea what my room looks like. Do you remember the Fall of the Roman Empire? Well, it looks like it fell on my room.

★   ★   ★

I don't have to straighten my room when my Mom tells me to. That would be considered cruel and unusual punishment.

★   ★   ★

My Mom doesn't push me to clean my room too much. Straightening my room is such a gigantic project, I would probably have to drop out of school to do it.

★   ★   ★

My room is so packed that I can't put any new junk in there until some of the old junk dies.

★   ★   ★

The mess in my room is very scientific. I can tell the age of some of my toys by how deep they are in the pile.

★   ★   ★

Mom says, "You should put some of your things in the closet." That's a laugh. The closet makes my room look neat.

★   ★   ★

My Mom says, "Why don't you throw away some of the things you don't want?" I say, "Because the things I don't want are on the bottom. I can't get to them because they're covered by the things I do want."

★   ★   ★

My room is clean, though; there's no room for dirt.

★   ★   ★

My room is so full of junk, if I invite a friend to stay the night he has to bring his own space.

★   ★   ★

Mom says, "How do you find the toys you want?" I don't. I just open the door and whatever falls out, I play with.

. . . except when it's my sister who falls out.

★   ★   ★

The Bible says that "man is dust and unto dust he shall return." My Mom says that in my room, under my bed, someone is always either coming or going.

★   ★   ★

I like junk. My goal is to be like Noah and have two of everything in my room.

★   ★   ★

I think that my Mom plans to straighten up my room once and for all. She's learning how to drive a bulldozer.

★   ★   ★

WHAT'S ALL THIS ABOUT NEATNESS?

We have a kid in our class who is so neat he wears a shirt and tie all the time . . . even when he takes a shower.

★　★　★

A buddy of mine is so neat he has a crease in his trousers from his waist down to his shoes . . . even when he's wearing short pants.

★　★　★

I once handed in a spotless mathematics test and flunked. The teacher said neatness counts; but I didn't.

★　★　★

We have a kid in our class who can't stand a spot of any kind on his clothes. If he had been born a leopard, he would have sent his fur out to be dry-cleaned.

★   ★   ★

This kid is so neat, when he takes his shoes and socks off, his feet have a shine on them.

★   ★   ★

This kid shines his shoes every single day. That's all right, but on the bottoms?

★   ★   ★

This kid is so neat, you have to have your trousers pressed just to be his best friend.

★   ★   ★

This kid is so neat, when he eats finger foods, he uses someone else's fingers.

★   ★   ★

He keeps his school books so neat, you would think they hadn't been used all year. You think that about my school books, too, but that's because they *haven't* been used all year.

★   ★   ★

This kid doesn't have a grade. His homework is so neat when he hands it in, the teacher is afraid to mark it.

★   ★   ★

This guy is so neat, when he plays Little League, he won't slide into a base unless he puts down a plastic sheet first.

★   ★   ★

We have a girl in our class who is very neat, too. She brought a note from her mother once that said, "Please forgive Sarah for being absent from school yesterday. Her dress had a wrinkle."

★   ★   ★

This girl is really neat. She washes the soap before washing her hands.

★   ★   ★

This one girl's so neat that if she accidentally spills something, it's always on somebody else.

★   ★   ★

I know one girl who hates anything that's not neat. She can get a stain out of her clothes just by staring at it.

★   ★   ★

One girl in our class is so neat she always parts her hair perfectly straight. That's fine, but in her eyebrows?

★   ★   ★

This girl's neat about everything. You should see how nicely she covers her books. Her geography book comes to school looking better than I do.

★   ★   ★

HAND-ME-DOWN CLOTHES:

My Mom loves hand-me-downs. I was lucky to be born in my own birthday suit.

★　★　★

I wore hand-me-downs for so long, when I broke my arm they put my brother's old cast on it.

★　★　★

All I ever wore were hand-me-downs. I sometimes think the only reason I was born was so that the clothes wouldn't go to waste.

★　★　★

I was the third person to wear these clothes to school. My blue jeans knew the lessons better than I did.

★　★　★

Some of the hand-me-downs were so worn by the time I got them, the only thing that held them together was modesty.

* * *

The hand-me-down clothes look pretty good. That's because they're so old they've lost the will to wrinkle.

Mom always dresses me in hand-me-downs. My clothes are so old that when we study history, I'm dressed for the part.

Some of my clothes are older than the event we're studying.

My clothes are real hand-me-downs. When I take them off at night, they hang themselves in my brother's closet.

* * *

My teacher recognized one of my sweaters. She went to school with it.

* * *

I hate family hand-me-downs. It's embarrassing when your clothes are old enough to vote but you're not.

* * *

The only place I can go without wearing hand-me-downs is a nudist camp.

* * *

The clothes I wear are not really mine. When my older brother whistles, my sweater runs into his room.

★ ★ ★

Hand-me-downs are embarrassing. I've got lint in my pockets older than I am.

★ ★ ★

My clothes are so old I feel guilty every time I walk by the Good Will bin at the supermarket.

★ ★ ★

That's all I ever wear are leftovers. I dress like my dog eats.

★ ★ ★

I wear nothing but clothes my older brothers out-grew. It could be worse. I could have had all sisters.

★ ★ ★

I've only had one article of clothing that was my own—a sweater I got for Christmas. It turned out to be too big for me so my Mother gave it to my brother.

. . . I'll wear it when he outgrows it.

★ ★ ★

I'M SO UNLUCKY:

I'm so unlucky I once cut myself opening a package of band-aids.

*   *   *

I'm the kind of guy who can get a paper cut opening a get-well card.

*   *   *

I'm so unlucky I tore a hole in my best pair of pants and I wasn't even wearing them at the time.

*   *   *

I once called "Dial-A-Prayer" and you know what I got? An answering service.

*   *   *

I once broke a mirror and got seven years bad luck. When the seven years were over I was so happy I threw my hat in the air. It came down and broke a mirror.

*   *   *

If it wasn't for bad luck, I wouldn't have any luck at all.

★   ★   ★

I once bought a rabbit's foot for good luck. It kicked me.

★   ★   ★

Thirteen is my unlucky number. Especially since that's how many F's I got on my last report card.

★   ★   ★

I'm really unlucky. My parents bought me a wrist-watch that's water-proof, shock-proof, rust-proof. I had it three days and it caught fire.

★   ★   ★

I have a friend who is so lucky he always comes up smelling like roses. I'm so unlucky, I just come up smelling.

I'm the unluckiest guy on earth. I'm probably the only guy who ever fell in while trying to toss a coin into a wishing well.

. . . I didn't even get my wish. My wish was that I didn't fall in.

. . . However, I did get my coin back.

. . . I figured as long as I was down there . . .

I'm so unlucky when a black cat crosses my path, the cat has bad luck.

★   ★   ★

4.
HARD TIMES
IN SCHOOL

TOUGH TEACHERS:

Boy, do I have a tough instructor. She has a black belt in teaching.

★   ★   ★

You know you're in for a rough year when you show up on the first day of school and your teacher has a Mr. T haircut.

. . . and she's a woman.

★   ★   ★

I had a real tough teacher once. On the first day of school she told us exactly how she was going to run her classroom. Then she gave us a little reward—smelling salts.

★   ★   ★

I once had a teacher who was so tough he was frightening, but I learned a lot in his class. I learned how to stutter.

★   ★   ★

> I have a teacher who is so tough, on the first day of class we all got the same grade—"F" for "frightened."
>
> . . . except for one kid who got an "A"— for "absolutely terrified."

One teacher I had was a tough disciplinarian. If she had taught King Kong in school, he would have turned out to be a nice gorilla.

★   ★   ★

Talk about tough teachers. One kid was caught chewing gum in this one teacher's room. She kept him in class and sent his teeth to the Principal's office.

★   ★   ★

One teacher was so tough: When he said "Be seated," the seat of the desk would jump up and meet you halfway.

★   ★   ★

I have one teacher who's really tough. You never tell this teacher you don't have your homework done. It's much easier to run away and join the Marines.

★   ★   ★

I have the toughest teacher in the world. In most classes you bring an apple for the teacher? With this teacher you bring raw meat.

★   ★   ★

This one woman was the toughest teacher I ever had. A lot of teachers make you bring your parents to school, but she kept them.

★   ★   ★

I had one real tough teacher whose penmanship was beautiful, which was surprising. It's hard to write well with an iron fist.

★   ★   ★

I had one teacher who gave out homework assignments that were so tough, you almost had to drop out of school to have time to complete them.

★   ★   ★

I had one tough teacher: During the summer months he generally found work as the warden of a Turkish prison.

★   ★   ★

I had a real tough teacher once. Everybody in her class learned to read quickly. That's because we all wanted to know what her tattoos said.

★   ★   ★

I once had a real no-nonsense teacher. When she called the roll, even kids who were absent said "Here."

★   ★   ★

One of my teachers had everybody scared. At Open House all the parents who came to her room brought a body guard.

★   ★   ★

HOMEWORK:

I don't understand it. We've only been back to school one week and I'm already three weeks behind in my homework.

★　★　★

Fair is fair. If I have to do schoolwork at home, I think my teacher should have to come to my house and make my bed every day.

★　★　★

There's only one thing worse than homework, and that's telling the teacher that you didn't do it.

★　★　★

One kid told the teacher that his dog ate his homework. The teacher flunked him and the dog.

★　★　★

I learned a good trick about homework from my father. If any words are misspelled, I blame them on my secretary.

★   ★   ★

One kid in our class has never missed or been late with one single homework assignment. The rest of the class was so proud of him that we chipped in and bought him a television set.

★   ★   ★

All my Mom and Dad ever ask me is: "Is your homework done?" After I graduate, my parents and I will have nothing left to talk about.

★   ★   ★

My teacher said, "You have two days to complete all your homework assignments." I said, "Good, I'll take Easter Sunday and New Year's."

★   ★   ★

One homework problem said, "If six men can dig a hole in two hours, how long would it take three men to dig the same hole?" I said, "Since the hole is already dug, why don't those three men put down their shovels and just help me finish my homework?"

★   ★   ★

The teacher said, "Where is your homework?" I said, "My dog ate it." The teacher said, "Where is your dog?" I said, "He's at the veterinarian's. My spelling makes him sick, too."

★   ★   ★

One teacher gives us so much work to take home, I had to add a spare room onto my school bag.

★   ★   ★

The teacher told one kid, "You're going to flunk this subject because you haven't finished your homework assignments." The kid said, "Good. I flunked all the other ones because I'm stupid."

★   ★   ★

I don't know why it's so important to finish your homework. As soon as you get it done, they just give you more.

★   ★   ★

Ever since I've been going to school, I have to do homework every night after dinner. I remember the good old days when all I used to get after dinner was dessert.

★   ★   ★

I can't win. If my teacher doesn't give me any homework for the night, my mother makes me do the dishes.

★   ★   ★

If I had my life to live over again, I wouldn't have time to finish all my homework.

★   ★   ★

My teacher asked, "What do you want to be when you grow up?" I said, "Caught up on all my homework."

★   ★   ★

I don't have any money yet, but I have enough homework to last me through my old age.

★   ★   ★

47

TESTS:

The teacher says he gives us tests to see how much we know. Except in my case, it's usually to see how much I don't know.

★   ★   ★

When I take a test, I don't put my name on the paper. If I have to guess how long it's going to take a train travelling 70 miles an hour to get from Point A to Point B, then let the teacher guess who's taking the test.

★   ★   ★

I'm really good at spelling. There are some words I can spell five or six different ways.

★   ★   ★

If teachers are supposed to be so smart, how come they're the only ones who get a book with all the answers in it?

★   ★   ★

Our teacher said, "Put your name in the upper right-hand corner of the paper and put the date in the upper left-hand corner of the paper." If he had stopped there I would have gotten 100 on the exam.

★   ★   ★

Our teacher said, "The questions on this exam are not difficult." I knew that. It's the answers that give me trouble.

★   ★   ★

The teacher said, "This test today will be multiple choice; what more do you want?" I said, "More choices."

★   ★   ★

I flunked a multiple choice exam and the teacher got very upset with me. I said, "It's your fault. You're the one who put down so many wrong answers."

★   ★   ★

The teacher said to me, "How can you not know George Washington's birthday?" I said, "He never remembers my birthday; so I'm not going to remember his."

★   ★   ★

The teacher asked on the test: "How many planets are in the sky?" I wrote down: "All of them."

★   ★   ★

I told my teacher I get nervous when I take a test. My hand shakes. He said, "You must have been very nervous during the geography test. You shook the Nile River out of Africa and clear over to Australia."

★ ★ ★

The teacher asked one kid to name two cities that were in Kentucky. He said, "Okay, I'll name one Dave and the other one Irving."

★ ★ ★

The teacher asked one student, "Where do we find the Suez Canal?" The student said, "It should be written right here on my sleeve with the rest of the answers."

★ ★ ★

The test asked: "If we have two straight lines that never meet, what do we call them?" I wrote: "Pretty unfriendly."

★ ★ ★

The teacher wanted to know when George Washington died. One kid had the answer. He said, "A few days before they buried him."

★ ★ ★

The teacher said, "What number comes after 4?" The kid answered, "All the rest of them."

★ ★ ★

The teacher said to me, "You got a perfect zero on your exam. How do you do it?" I said, "It was just luck. I guessed at a few of the answers."

★ ★ ★

THE SMART KID IN CLASS:

We have a kid in our class who is real smart. He considers "A−" a flunking grade.

★   ★   ★

This one kid is so smart that during tests the teacher copies from him.

★   ★   ★

I have a friend who's got more brains in his little finger than I have in my entire body. I know because his little finger gets higher grades than I do.

★   ★   ★

I know one guy who's the smartest kid in the whole school. He gets higher grades than the rest of us—even on tests that he doesn't show up for.

★ ★ ★

I have one friend who's so smart that the rest of us have to study just to copy from her.

★ ★ ★

This one friend of mine is so smart, he wins the school spelling bee every year. He knows how to spell words that the rest of us get a headache just looking at.

★ ★ ★

This one kid is so smart he gets all "A's" in school. The last time he got a "B" was in kindergarten. He fell a little behind in "sandbox."

THE AIR-BRAIN:

One kid in our class is such an air-brain he threw his bike away because the back wheel kept going frontwards.

     ★   ★   ★

I have a classmate who's such an air-brain, when he gets amnesia he actually gets smarter.

     ★   ★   ★

One kid I knew was such an air-brain he had his address tattooed on his forehead. That way, when he got lost he could mail himself home.

     ★   ★   ★

One kid was such an air-brain he was late for school one day because he put his shoes on the wrong feet. Then he couldn't remember whose feet he put them on.

     ★   ★   ★

I know one air-brain who invented a pencil with an eraser at both ends. He said it was for people who make the same mistake twice.

     ★   ★   ★

One friend of mine had to take the I.Q. test twice to get it up to a whole number.

*　　*　　*

This one kid I know is so slow he took his dog to obedience school. The dog passed; he flunked.

*　　*　　*

When they were giving out brains, this stupid kid thought they said "trains" and said, "Give me one that goes around in circles."

*　　*　　*

This other kid is so stupid he once tried to jump across a well in two jumps.

*　　*　　*

This one friend I have may be the stupidest. His mouth was all sore last week because he's so dumb. I told him, "Next time, seal the envelopes *before* you put them in the mailbox."

*　　*　　*

I know one guy who's so stupid, he flunks exams even when he cheats. Last week he wrote all the answers on his sleeve, then at the last minute he remembered he can't read.

*　　*　　*

I know one stupid kid whose mother once bought him some "Silly Putty" to play with. It outsmarted him.

*　　*　　*

THE KID WHO'S ALWAYS IN TROUBLE:

We had a kid in our class who spent so much time in the Principal's office, they gave him his own key.

★　　★　　★

This classmate of mine spent so much time in the Principal's office, if the Principal got sick, this kid could fill in for him.

★　　★　　★

A buddy of mine was always in trouble. His parents were called to the school so often, they had a better attendance record than he did.

★　　★　　★

One kid in our class was always in trouble. I won't say his parents were called into school often, but his Mom and Dad had the lead in the school play.

★ ★ ★

One kid I knew was always in trouble at school. Every teacher would say, "I want to see your parents." He didn't realize he was a bad kid; he just thought his Mom and Dad were very popular.

★ ★ ★

This one kid I knew got in trouble so easily, he was kept after school even on days when he was absent.

★ ★ ★

One of my classmates was kept after school so much that his parents finally rented out his room.

★ ★ ★

I knew one guy who was kept after school so much they finally hired him as the janitor. They figured as long as he was going to be there at night anyway, he might as well mop the floors.

★ ★ ★

I had one school mate who had to write "I will not misbehave" on the blackboard so many times, he had to rent blackboard space from another school.

★ ★ ★

One friend of mine is in so much trouble he has to stay after school for seven years after he graduates.

OTHER WEIRD CHARACTERS:

I have some funny-looking friends. One guy, his ears are so big that his head looks like a Volkswagen with the doors open.

★   ★   ★

One of them is bowlegged and he goes with a girl who is knock-kneed. When they walk down the street together they spell "OX."

★   ★   ★

One friend of mine wears such ratty clothes, he has to repair them to throw them away.

★   ★   ★

This kid is the worst dresser in the world. His favorite color is "mildew."

★   ★   ★

One of my buddies is totally lazy. The last time this kid worked up a sweat, his mother didn't wash his work shirt; she framed it.

This kid is really lazy. They have dolls out now that do more than he does.

He's too lazy to even set his clock. He just waits until it's an hour off and then moves to another time zone.

It takes him forever to read a book. He keeps waiting for the wind to turn the pages.

This other friend of mine is so boring, at parties, he stays in the room with the coats.

. . . and sometimes a few of the coats leave.

He's so boring, he has a pet turtle who gets invited to more parties than he does.

His favorite pastime is sitting on the sidewalk and watching cement harden.

He's so dull, he has the personality of a lawn chair. He just sits there and rusts.

No one likes to be with him. When he goes to the beach, the tide goes out and stays there.

★   ★   ★

5.
EAT YOUR HEART OUT

MY SISTER'S BAD COOKING:

My sister is a terrible cook. When she cooks a meal, all the flies in the house buzz around the medicine chest.

★   ★   ★

After one of her meals, I went in the kitchen and saw a cockroach eating a Tum.

★   ★   ★

She can't even throw away the leftovers. She throws them in the garbage disposal; it throws them back.

★   ★   ★

She served a beautiful meal last night. Meat loaf in one corner of the plate, mashed potatoes in another corner of the plate, and brussels sprouts in another corner. She has to put them all in separate corners so we can tell them apart.

★   ★   ★

Our family believes in brushing between meals, but when my sister cooks, we brush during.

* * *

The other night a Chicken Delight truck came to the door. I went to answer it, but a mouse pushed me aside and said, "That's for me."

* * *

When Mom cooks we bring our friends to the house for dinner. When my sister cooks, we bring our enemies.

* * *

When she cooks, we don't say grace. We say the last rites.

* * *

In fact, sometimes when my sister cooks, if we're good all day, Mom will send us to bed without our supper. She's on Betty Crocker's most wanted list.

* * *

I think my sister is the worst cook in the world. Who else do you know who can burn Jell-O?

* * *

The other day she made breakfast for my Dad— coffee and toast. He had to scrape both of them.

* * *

What my sister usually makes is stew. It always starts out to be something else, though.

* * *

Once my sister burned my mother's favorite pot. It looked terrible, but it tasted better than the meal.

* * *

When my sister cooks, lockjaw seems like a blessing.

★ ★ ★

When my sister cooks we don't have to eat everything on our plates. Dad has a rule that we don't have to eat anything we can't identify.

★ ★ ★

My sister took a cooking class and the only "A" she got was in "ptomaine."

★ ★ ★

My Mom has a card in our medicine chest that tells how to treat different poisons. Six of my sister's recipes are listed there.

★ ★ ★

My brothers and I like her hamburgers. We use them for hockey pucks.

★ ★ ★

My sister made a batch of cookies once that were so hard we paved our driveway with them.

★ ★ ★

TABLE MANNERS:

My kid brother has worse table manners than an orangutan. At least an orangutan has sense enough to stay out of restaurants.

★　　★　　★

Before meals he doesn't say grace—he says a victory prayer.

★　　★　　★

Grace for him goes: "Thank you, Lord, for bringing this food in. Now let's eat, and may the better man win."

★　　★　　★

His table manners are so bad his knife and fork are registered with the authorities as dangerous weapons.

★　　★　　★

When my kid brother eats, he doesn't use etiquette; he uses a battle plan.

★　　★　　★

He sucks his food down so fast that the potatoes on my plate start spinning.

★   ★   ★

He generally has more food running down his chin than most other people have on their plate.

★   ★   ★

At meal time, my kid brother considers table manners a sign of weakness.

★   ★   ★

Some people learn their manners from Emily Post; he learned his from Attila the Hun.

★   ★   ★

Eating with this kid is like sitting down to a meal in front of the kitchen sink and watching the garbage disposal operate.

★   ★   ★

He eats so fast the only time he chews his food is when he's trying to kill time.

★   ★   ★

He eats so fast his nickname is "the human vacuum cleaner."

★   ★   ★

He eats soup like an unclogged drain.

★   ★   ★

He considers mashed potatoes a finger food.

★   ★   ★

He's good to bring along on a picnic, though. His eating habits are so bad that even the ants stay away.

★   ★   ★

IN THE SOUP:

My Mom used to make chicken soup that was like a medicine. It never cured anything, but it tasted like castor oil.

★   ★   ★

I have a friend who's so organized he eats his alphabet soup in alphabetical order.

I asked him once why he did that. He said, "In case I get interrupted during lunch, I'll know where I left off."

★   ★   ★

When my uncle ate soup, sea-lions used to come into our kitchen. He'd slurp so loud that seals would mistake it for their mating call.

★   ★   ★

My brother's tie had so many food stains on it, if you boiled it you could make soup.

*   *   *

This one restaurant we went to used to make soup that was so greasy, if you sprinkled salt and pepper on it, they slid right off.

*   *   *

Their soup was so greasy you had to eat it with a non-skid spoon.

*   *   *

I asked one waiter, "What's your soup like today?" He said, "just like it was yesterday only a day older."

*   *   *

They advertise a soup that will put color back in your cheeks. They don't tell you that the color is green.

*   *   *

Their soup is so greasy you can either eat it here or take it with you and put it in the crankcase of your car.

*   *   *

Their soup is so greasy they're only allowed to serve it in the "no-smoking" section of the restaurant.

*   *   *

This other restaurant makes soup that's like water—only not as thick.

*   *   *

Soup is a very good food, but it makes a lousy sandwich.

*   *   *

TOTALLY NUTS:

There was a kid in my street we used to call "Hershey Bar with Almonds." He was half nuts.

★ ★ ★

This kid I knew used to love peanuts. He had six scrapbooks full of them.

★ ★ ★

One kid in our class was mean. He used to tape peanuts to the inside of the window just to drive the pigeons nuts.

★ ★ ★

My brother is so cheap, he likes to go to the park and *sell* peanuts to the pigeons.

★ ★ ★

My little brother ate so many bags of peanuts at the ballpark that by the end of the game he knew how to climb trees.

. . . with his tail.

★   ★   ★

My little brother puts peanut butter on everything—the refrigerator door, the sofa, the new carpeting . . .

★   ★   ★

My little brother loves peanuts. If he had been born a monkey, he'd not only be happier, but also better-looking.

He'd also be useful for getting our kite down when it's stuck in a tree.

★   ★   ★

My little brother loves peanuts so much he took a bag of peanut shells to the grocery store and said, "Fill 'em up."

★   ★   ★

My cousin's allergic to nuts—all kind of nuts. She can't even go to family reunions.

★   ★   ★

Did you hear about the shy peanut who will probably live forever? He refuses to come out of his shell.

★   ★   ★

6.
DISASTER DAYS

VALENTINE'S DAY:

I used to send Valentine cards, but only to girls who hadn't learned how to read yet.

★　　★　　★

One year I received 286 Valentine's cards. I would have gotten more, but my hand got tired writing out my address.

★　　★　　★

I know a girl that got 28 Valentines from secret admirers. No one she knew would admit that they liked her.

★　　★　　★

One year I got a strange Valentine. It said: "I've always admired you from afar. Stay there."

★　　★　　★

One Valentine's Day, I got a nice message. It said: "Would you please spend some time with me after school?" Unfortunately, it was from the Principal.

★　　★　　★

HALLOWEEN:

I don't think Halloween is such a scary day. Now final exams—that's scary.

★ ★ ★

Halloween is one night when kids scare adults by getting dressed as somebody else. The rest of the year we scare adults just by being ourselves.

★ ★ ★

I don't like Halloween. Once I won the funniest costume award and I just went to the party to pick up my little brother.

★ ★ ★

I don't like to wear complicated costumes for Halloween. I just carry my brother's report card and go trick or treating as a student with passing grades.

★ ★ ★

One fellow in our class was so dumb, on Halloween he used to carve a face in an apple and go bobbing for pumpkins.

★   ★   ★

One kid in our class was so skinny, he had to put on weight to get dressed as a skeleton.

★   ★   ★

One girl in our class is so skinny, she put on a fuzzy white hat and fuzzy white slippers and went out as a Q-tip.

★   ★   ★

Another kid in our class is so heavy, he just wears a grey suit and goes trick or treating as a battleship.

★   ★   ★

Another kid in our class is short and heavy. For Halloween, he just painted himself red, white, and blue and stood on the corner as a mailbox.

★   ★   ★

One kid in our class was so weird-looking he used to make money posing for Halloween masks.

★   ★   ★

One kid had a devil's costume that looked so real, four kids on our block sold their souls to him.

★   ★   ★

One kid came to our Halloween party with a sheet thrown over his head. I said, "What're you supposed to be—a ghost?" He said, "No. An unmade bed."

★   ★   ★

One year we had too many kids at our Halloween party, so we made all the kids dressed as pirates walk the plank.

★   ★   ★

One year, we had so many kids come dressed as pirates that our Halloween party ended early. Everybody got seasick.

★   ★   ★

One kid came to our Halloween party with a realistic looking vampire costume. That put an end to the kissing games we were going to play.

★   ★   ★

This kid really thought he was a vampire. When we bobbed for apples, he'd bite into them and suck out all the juice.

★   ★   ★

One of my friends got dressed as a girl for Halloween. He looked so good that this Saturday night he's got a date with himself.

★   ★   ★

Last Halloween my best buddy wore a mouse costume. It was so real-looking my cat ate him.

★   ★   ★

CHRISTMAS:

On the first Christmas, the three wise men brought gifts of gold, frankincense, myrrh, and some batteries to operate them.

★   ★   ★

I know some parents who were smart. For Christmas they gave their children a whole boxful of batteries. On the side of the box was written: "Toys not included."

★   ★   ★

My parents gave me a chess game that I can't beat. Just what I wanted for Christmas—a game that's smarter than I am.

★   ★   ★

The stores get real crowded around Christmas time. I went to do some shopping the other day, and the store was so packed, when I came out I had three tattoos I didn't have when I went in.

★   ★   ★

I went Christmas shopping and was surprised at the crowds. I walked four blocks and my feet never touched the ground.

★   ★   ★

The store was so crowded it was like a sardine can with Christmas wreaths hanging in it.

★   ★   ★

I said to one person, "This is the most crowded I've ever seen this elevator." He said, "What elevator? Someone stuffed the both of us in a shopping bag."

★   ★   ★

The store was so crowded, I sneezed and three aisles over some lady's hat flew off.

★   ★   ★

My Dad went Christmas shopping and I said, "Don't forget to buy me something." He said, "Buy me, buy me, buy me. It's Christmas time. You should think of giving." I said, "Okay. Buy me a gift, and then give it to me."

★   ★   ★

One year my mother bought me a plaything that was guaranteed unbreakable. I used it to break all my other toys.

★   ★   ★

I hate toys that say, "Some assembly required." By the time you put them together, you're too old to play with them.

★   ★   ★

One kid on our block was very good with Legos. He built his parents a summer home in Connecticut.

★   ★   ★

I always had bad luck with toys. I had the only rubber ducky in the world that couldn't float.

★   ★   ★

I had a teddy bear that was supposed to keep me company when I went to sleep. It was afraid of the dark.

I didn't care. I had to get rid of it anyway. It used to hog all the covers.

★   ★   ★

I even had an invisible friend that everyone could see but me.

★   ★   ★

My sister had a Barbie Doll, but she hated it. My parents bought it better clothes than they bought her.

She didn't have much luck with toys. Her Barbie Doll joined a nudist camp.

★   ★   ★

Toys teach you things that you'll use when you grow up. When I go to college, I plan to major in Mr. Slinky.

★   ★   ★

I had a buddy who had relatives in Australia. They sent him a boomerang. He didn't like it, but every time he tried to throw it away, he hurt himself.

★   ★   ★

NEW YEAR'S

I don't have to make any New Year's resolutions this year. Luckily, I never got around to any of the ones I made last year.

★   ★   ★

Last year I resolved to practice the piano faithfully for one hour a day. Tomorrow I'll be right on schedule—provided I play the piano for 78 hours.

★   ★   ★

Once I resolved never again to make up fantastic excuses for not doing my homework. I would have kept it, too, except a Martian space ship landed in my room and their dog ate all my homework assignments.

★   ★   ★

My buddies and I always try to make resolutions that are easy to keep. Like last year I resolved not to play ice hockey in July.

. . . or to go snorkeling in November.

. . . or to beat Arnold Schwarzenegger in arm wrestling.

★　★　★

I really like New Year's Day. It's the only day of the year that I'm not behind in my homework.

★　★　★

7.
TIME OUT FOR GOOD BEHAVIOR

TRAVELLING:

We stay at some pretty crummy places when we go travelling. At one place, the rooms were so small, when you went inside your shadow had to wait for you outside.

We stayed in one cottage that was so small you had to step outside to change your mind.

★   ★   ★

This room was so small, the only way you could open the closet door was from outside the room.

One place advertised a swimming hole, but you had to bring your own water.

★   ★   ★

One place we stayed had two types of cottages. They both had running water, but in the more expensive ones, the water came out of faucets.

★   ★   ★

One place had screen doors and windows that were falling apart. The only things those screens kept out were the people who had rented the cottage last year.

In one place the mosquitoes were so large you never knew if they were going to bite you there or carry you off and have you later for a snack.

I never saw such big mosquitoes. They looked like owls with pointy noses.

Those critters were really big. When's the last time you saw a mosquito with landing gear?

. . . and bomb sights?

★   ★   ★

When we got home, my mother said, "You're sunburned." I said, "No. I'm just red from slapping mosquitoes for two weeks."

We've stayed at some nice places, too. At one hotel the towels were so fluffy, Dad could hardly close our suitcases.

★   ★   ★

SUMMER CAMP:

Last year at camp I went for a short walk in the woods. Then I saw a snake and it became a short run in the woods.

★ ★ ★

I go away to summer camp every year. Mosquitoes have to eat, too.

★ ★ ★

I'm not a real outdoor type. I break out in poison ivy just from going to see the movie, *Bambi.*

★ ★ ★

When I went to summer camp, I got poison ivy on parts of my body I never knew I had before.

★ ★ ★

I go to a very tame summer camp. The only wild animals there are the adult counselors.

★ ★ ★

My first day at camp, the counselor asked, "What would you like to get out of summer camp this year?" I said, "Me."

     ★   ★   ★

I made a lot of new friends at camp— unfortunately, they were all frogs.

     ★   ★   ★

Every night kids would put different things in my sleeping bag as a joke. Going to bed was like having a pajama party with green things.

     ★   ★   ★

Noah had two of everything on his ark. I think I had the same thing last night in my sleeping bag.

     ★   ★   ★

One kid said, "What's green and slimy and has over 200 legs?" I said, "I don't know." He said, "I don't know, either, but a couple of them just crawled into your sleeping bag."

     ★   ★   ★

I've had just about everything in my sleeping bag except a good night's sleep.

     ★   ★   ★

Summer camp is educational. Last year I learned how to say "Help" underwater.

     ★   ★   ★

I felt sorry for one kid. His parents sent him to summer camp and then moved.

     ★   ★   ★

NOT GOOD AT SPORTS:

I'm not very good at sports. The first time I caught a cold I dropped it.

★   ★   ★

I figure if God wanted us to catch things, He would have given us hands made of Velcro.

★   ★   ★

It takes me a long time to run to first base. That's because I have to stop and ask directions.

★   ★   ★

If we play a choose-up game on Sunday, I don't get picked until around Tuesday.

★   ★   ★

I only caught one pop-up in my entire life. Unfortunately, it was one that I had hit also.

★   ★   ★

Usually, when they play baseball, they put the worst player in right field. The last time we played, they put me in Iowa.

★   ★   ★

I can't catch. I know that everything that goes up must come down, but I don't want it to come down anywhere near me.

★   ★   ★

I never catch anything. I've had this mitt for four years, and so far, the only thing that's been in it is my hand.

★   ★   ★

The guys kid me about being uncoordinated. They say I not only have two left feet, but they're both on backwards.

★   ★   ★

I've only hit one home run in my entire life. Unfortunately, we were playing football at the time.

★ ★ ★

Some kids can't chew gum and walk at the same time. I have trouble doing them separately.

★ ★ ★

I'm not real good at athletics. Even when I try to read the sports page, I drop it.

★ ★ ★

I may be the only kid in school who's flunking recess.

★ ★ ★

My Mom came to see me play in my first Little League game. In the third inning she sent in a pinch-mother.

8.
IT'S ALL OVER BUT THE SCREAMING

DOCTORS:

There are two places I hate to go more than any other place in the world. One is the doctor's office, and so is the other one.

★   ★   ★

Every time I go to my doctor he gives me another needle. I don't mind so much when I'm sick, but last week I was just delivering a package.

★   ★   ★

I've gotten so many needles from my doctor, when the wind blows up my sleeve, my arm whistles.

★   ★   ★

My doctor has given me so many needles I may never get sick again. If any germ gets into my body it will fall out through one of the thousands of little holes in my skin.

★   ★   ★

My doctor is bad at giving needles, too. He's got all these diplomas on his wall, but not a single one for marksmanship.

★ ★ ★

The last time I went, the doctor looked in my ears, up my nose, and down my throat. I said, "Doctor, if you tell me what you're looking for, I'll tell you where I keep it."

Once I went to him with something in my eye. He said, "Did your mother ever have something in her eye?" I said, "Yes." He said, "Did your father ever have something in his eye?" I said, "Yes." He said, "There's your problem. It runs in the family."

★ ★ ★

If he's such a good doctor, how come everybody in his waiting room is sick?

★ ★ ★

The doctor's waiting room actually cured one guy. He went there with a case of amnesia and stayed in the waiting room so long, he forgot he had it.

★   ★   ★

I used to go to a baby doctor, but he grew up.

The last doctor I went to kept feeling my nose. Then we found out he was a veterinarian.

I figured that out when the prescription he wrote was for "Kibbles and Bits."

I'm just glad we found out before he got around to the flea bath.

All the medicine my doctor gives me tastes terrible. I'm glad he became a doctor, and not a cook.

★   ★   ★

Once I had the 24-hour flu. He gave me a medicine that tasted bad for 72 hours.

★   ★   ★

The doctor said, "How long have you had this problem?" I said, "Two days." He said, "Why didn't you come see me sooner?" I said, "I did. That's how long I've been in your waiting room."

★   ★   ★

DENTISTS:

I went to the dentist yesterday and he didn't hurt me at all. I think he would have if he ever caught me, though.

    ★   ★   ★

I'm a coward. When my dentist asks if I want novocaine, I say, "Yes, and throw in a blindfold while you're at it."

    ★   ★   ★

I can't stand pain. I ask for novocaine when I get my hair cut.

    ★   ★   ★

Did you ever get novocaine? It feels like a whole side of your face is a balloon in the Macy's Thanksgiving Day Parade.

    ★   ★   ★

Novocaine deadens your whole face. If you try to smile, the only thing that moves is your ears.

    ★   ★   ★

My dentist said, "Let me know if I hurt you." I said, "Doctor, I'm going to let everybody know if you hurt me."

★   ★   ★

My dentist said, "I didn't know you had a gold filling." I said, "I don't. You've drilled so deep you hit my belt buckle."

My dentist put some cotton in my mouth, then he put in some instruments, then more cotton, then more instruments, then more cotton. I said, "Doctor, do you plan to fix my teeth, or move in?"

I know one patient who said to the dentist, "Doctor, I think you've pulled the wrong tooth." The dentist looked in again and said, "No, I pulled the right tooth. You got the cavity in the wrong one."

Then the dentist said, "Look on the bright side. If this tooth ever does go bad, you won't have to have it pulled again."

★   ★   ★

This dentist looked in his patient's mouth and said, "Your teeth are fine. Your gums are going to have to come out."

★   ★   ★

GROUCHY NEIGHBORS:

We have a neighbor who is old, cranky, and can't get along with anyone. He has arthritis of the personality.

★   ★   ★

Our neighbor is a real grouch. The kindest thing ever to come out of her mouth is laryngitis.

★   ★   ★

Another neighbor is so nasty, when she comes out in the morning to pick up her milk, it curdles.

★   ★   ★

We have the grouchiest neighbor in the world. She tore down her picket fence and put up sandbags.

★   ★   ★

This neighbor is so grouchy her dog put up a sign that says, "Beware of Owner."

I think we have the grouchiest neighbor in the world. She makes the Wicked Witch of the West look like Snow White.

★   ★   ★

She is really mean. She has the world's only man-eating welcome mat.

★   ★   ★

Everybody is afraid of our grouchy neighbor. Even the people who deliver the newspaper won't go near the house. They call her on the phone and read the morning paper to her.

★   ★   ★

Even the mail carriers won't go near her. They roll her mail up in little balls and shoot them at her through a pea shooter.

Everybody in the neighborhood hates this one grouchy neighbor. They say she has the only house on the block with a two-broom garage.

★   ★   ★

She is such a grouch Mother Theresa wanted to punch her in the nose.

★   ★   ★

There's one lady on our block who is so mean, the dentist charges her extra. Apparently, fangs are harder to work on.

★   ★   ★

We have one neighbor who's a terror. If she moved into Mr. Rogers' Neighborhood, Mr. McFeeley would move out.

★   ★   ★

When this one grouchy neighbor yells at us kids, everything runs away from her house. It's the first time I ever saw snails leave skid marks.

★   ★   ★

INDEX